PAMPHLETS ON AMERICAN WRITERS • NUMBER 86

UNIVERSITY OF MINNESOTA

˄ *Isaac Bashevis Singer*

BY BEN SIEGEL

UNIVERSITY OF MINNESOTA PRESS · MINNEAPOLIS

Printed in the United States of America at
the North Central Publishing Company, St. Paul

Library of Congress Catalog Card Number: 74-628289

PUBLISHED IN GREAT BRITAIN, INDIA, AND PAKISTAN BY THE OXFORD
UNIVERSITY PRESS, LONDON, BOMBAY, AND KARACHI, AND IN CANADA
BY THE COPP CLARK PUBLISHING CO. LIMITED, TORONTO

ISAAC BASHEVIS SINGER

BEN SIEGEL, critic, reviewer, and editor, is a professor of English at California State Polytechnic College, Pomona. Among his books are *The Puritan Heritage: America's Roots in the Bible and Biography Past and Present.*

⌄ Isaac Bashevis Singer

A RECENT literary surprise has been the incursion into American letters of a Polish-born Yiddish novelist only a few years younger than the century. Alone of Yiddish writers, Isaac Bashevis Singer has caught the fancy of critics, teachers, students, and public. His closest rival for this distinction would be Sholem Asch, whose novels sold widely in the United States in the 1930's and 1940's. But Asch never garnered Singer's critical acclaim.

Singer's fame was overdue. For two decades only a dwindling Yiddish readership knew he existed. He lived in America for fifteen years before having a book, *The Family Moskat* (1950), published in English. His new audience formed with *Satan in Goray* (1955) and *Gimpel the Fool and Other Stories* (1957). Now even his earliest works are in paperback. He has won several awards, the quarterlies run articles on his fiction, and the weeklies review him as an important "American" writer. One month in the late 1960's saw five of his tales in as many major magazines and journals. Each new book broadens, even when it doesn't enhance, his literary reputation. Five novels, four collections of tales, four slender volumes for children, and one series of autobiographical sketches are now in English. Three long novels (*The Estate, Shadows by the Hudson, A Ship to America*) await translation, as do three shorter ones (*Enemies — A Love Story, The Certificate,* and *The Charlatan*).

Wary of his new fame, Singer views the Yiddish writer in America as living in the past, "a ghost . . . [who] sees others but is himself not seen." This is hard to refute. Yet his own fiction evokes a past rich in the sufferings and joys, shapes and sounds of

5

the Jewish exile's last four centuries. His dybbuks and beggars, rabbis and atheists, saints and whores are bound by common spiritual ties, an expressive common tongue, a common destiny, and frequently a common martyrdom. Together they constitute the most varied and coherent cavalcade of Jewish life in modern fiction.

Singer is no primitive. Despite exotic materials and idiomatic style, he is a sophisticated craftsman with the easy fluency attained by only the finest writers in any culture. He is a born storyteller, with sure insight and an outrageous compulsion to create. Fable and fantasy, chronicle and saga, tale and essay issue from his pen. His least inspired tales have a tender, gusty, tragic vitality derived from a sensitive fusion of Yiddish and Western traditions. His little people's pieties and lusts evoke the stark realities not only of Gogol and Dostoevski, Isaac Babel and Isaac Loeb Peretz, but of Nathaniel Hawthorne and William Faulkner. He rejects any claim that imagination cannot compete with reality. All men are hedonists, he declares, and they expect literature to provide enjoyment and information; thus a writer does well to concentrate on "real stories" while avoiding mood pieces and obscurities. "One Kafka in a century is enough," he states. "A whole army of Kafkas could destroy literature." A veteran journalist, Singer has a healthy respect for the hard fact and objective report. Yet he sees perversity and originality in all existence; "everything alive," he points out, is unique, singular, and non-repeatable. Those "realistic" writers who reduce all creation to the near and familiar only end up sounding alike. Fiction mirrors God's artistry, Singer believes, only when facts are extended and enlarged by images from the unconscious or supernatural. This fusion of fact and image, of objective report and subjective fancy, he terms chronicle — "external chronicle and psychological chronicle."

Isaac Bashevis Singer

Singer's knowledge of Jewish psyche and culture is deep, certain, ancestral. One of the few writers to have mastered the entire Judaic tradition, he can enter and articulate it at any point without a discordant note. So true are eye, ear, and verbal touch that tone and mood are often the major conveyers of meaning. Viewing traditional concepts and values with an ambiguous mixture of love, pride, and doubt, he finds no easy answers to the eternal questions. What few answers there are, he makes clear, each must glean for himself. His refusal to champion group, philosophy, or commandment bothers many. For Singer all mankind constitutes the human reality; hence he spares neither Jew nor Christian, code nor attitude.

From an Orthodox background, with rabbis on both sides of the family, Singer (born in 1904) read no secular literature until he was twelve. His older brother was Israel Joshua Singer, author of *Yoshe Kalb* and *The Brothers Ashkenazi*. Both rejected rabbinical careers to champion the *Haskala* or Jewish Enlightenment. Their sister, Esther Kreitman, was also a novelist. Singer leans heavily on this rich heritage. His literary world is the circumscribed but rich one of Polish Jewry from the seventeenth to the twentieth century. Now gone, its vestiges cremated or obliterated, this world has been reshaped in his fiction by an adroit mingling of Hasidic and cabalist thought, demonology and Cossack massacres, the Sabbatian heresy and the Enlightenment.

Singer writes only in Yiddish, a language experiencing steady attrition if not extinction. Most of his work appears first in the *Jewish Daily Forward*, to which he has contributed since his arrival in America in 1935. He has been a *Forward* staff member since 1944 and also writes sketches for the paper's radio program on New York station WEVD. Singer enjoys thoroughly the "very good profession" of newspaper work, but he signs his journalistic fiction Isaac Warshawsky and does not publish it in book form.

7

His more serious work (appearing in the *Forward*'s weekend literary supplement) he signs Isaac Bashevis. When a journalistic piece turns out well, he may revise and publish it under his own name. His fiction rarely reveals concern over his shrinking Yiddish audience; personal views are reserved for essay and lecture. If in these he admits the future of Yiddish appears "very black," he still insists the language is like the Jews themselves — who "die all the time and yet go on living."

Singer weaves into his fiction the motions, idiom, and humor of ghetto and small-town Jewish life, the *shtetl* life which was — if little else — integrated and coherent. His precise images lay bare the Jewish grain without pretense or shout. No aspect of life is too trivial or solemn to be reduced to bare motive. "I am," he confesses, "more fascinated by page four of the *Daily News* than I am by the front page of the *New York Times*." Aware of everything, he disdains little. Singer's characters do not perform great deeds; the world has crushed or bypassed them. Yet despite terror, suffering, disappointment, they accept and even love life, being determined to endure. Singer refuses to apologize for his material. His stance is that of the traditional tale-spinner whose listeners grasp every outlandish allusion, nuance, and inflection. East Europe's Jewish world becomes a familiar, continuing culture and its complex structure of beliefs, customs, and loyalties understandable commonplaces. Distance, time, and cultural change are bridged without forced reverie or nostalgia. Yet Singer feels keenly his peculiar situation. "When I sit down to write," he states, "I have the feeling that I'm talking maybe to millions and maybe to nobody." He need have little fear. The modern reader, non-Jew and Jew, finds himself responding to that strange, departed clime and becoming intensely involved with Singer's embattled little people who now seem very much like all men everywhere.

Singer's tough, intimate, earthy prose conveys the rhythms of Yiddish folk speech — its human beat and stress, intonations and embodied gestures. His frequently archaic, at times obsolete, Yiddish (discernible even in translation) reinforces a complex interweaving of fact and fantasy, comedy and terror. Like that of the last century's Yiddish masters — Mendele, Sholom Aleichem, Peretz — Singer's language exudes the verbal spontaneity and improvisation of a long oral tradition. Lucid, exact, penetrating, it conveys a human voice — "the swift, living voice," as Ted Hughes puts it, "of the oral style"; thus it proves a prime medium for expressing the Jewish communal code with its memories, hopes, and defeats. Above all, Singer's prose gives lie to the legend that Yiddish does not translate into English. He is pleased to be read in English, to have a "very real" audience rather than the "near-imaginary" Yiddish one. Still, forty percent of each book's value, Singer feels, is lost in translation, despite his personal involvement. He has translated Russian and German fiction into Yiddish and is aware of the difficulties. "Translation is an endless process," he states, with every work posing a unique problem. "Nevertheless, good translation is possible, but it involves hard work for the writer, the translator, and the editor. I don't think that a translation is ever really finished. To me the translation becomes as dear as the original."

His appalled conviction that English translators had mutilated Sholom Aleichem's writings precipitated a deep concern for his own work. His collaboration helps explain why early translators proved sensitive enough to his subtle nuances to attain unity of style and tone. To say Singer's lucid, pithy Yiddish finds ready English equivalents takes nothing from able craftsmen like Saul Bellow, Jacob Sloan, and Isaac Rosenfeld. Together they brought Singer to a large, appreciative audience and demonstrated the value of competent literary translation — an endeavor not lacking in deriders. His more recent successes in English, however, have been due to Singer himself: in the past few years he has translated his own books and stories. Those listed as "translators" merely edit his English syntax and grammar; most do not know more than a few Yiddish words.

Ironically, Yiddish critics do not rate Singer as high as do the English speaking. American readers find appealing his offbeat themes and rejection of social philosophies — in short, his existential stance; Yiddish readers, however, often view him with an uneasiness akin to suspicion. Several Yiddish critics have attacked his tales of "horror and eroticism," his "distasteful blend of superstition and shoddy mysticism," and his "pandering" to non-Jewish tastes. What merit these criticisms may have is vitiated by the obvious resentment accompanying them — a resentment that develops in some literary corners whenever a writer wins recognition beyond the Yiddish pale. Sholem Asch proved a similar target.

Yet Singer does have a perverse, if not morbid, taste for violence, blood, and animal slaughter, not to mention rape, demons, and the grave — all gothic horror story elements. He relishes those medieval superstitions and fears that clung to *shtetl* life into the twentieth century. His devils, demons, and imps may represent a partial deference to the strong contemporary taste for "black humor" in its myriad forms. But primarily his demonology enables Singer to expose the demons driving us all. His devils and imps symbolize those erratic, wayward, and diabolic impulses that detour men from their fathers' piety and morality. Singer's popularity is the more understandable at a time when such practitioners of the gothic and macabre as William Faulkner, William Styron, Flannery O'Connor, Tennessee Williams, and Edward Albee have won strong acceptance.

Many young readers today lack rapport or patience with the

"traditional" novel, or with any adherence to the older themes
and values. Singer's skepticism, his spiritual and psychological
openness, seem attuned to their own intellectual restlessness. But
Singer's integrity and imagination transcend mere fad or fashion.
His vision is as tragic as that of the Greek dramatists. He too sees
a universe governed by forces lying beyond reason or justice. For
man this often means neither certainty on earth nor concern in
heaven. "From a cabalistic point of view," he states, "I am a very
realistic writer. Cabalists believe there are millions of worlds, but
the worst is this one. Here is the very darkness itself." Singer
therefore is as convinced as were Hawthorne and Faulkner that
evil is so near and constant a danger no one can avoid profaning
life's most sacred aspects. Not for Singer, then, a facile romantic
optimism. He has few illusions about man's ability or desire to
better the world or himself. "My judgment is that good does not
always triumph," he asserts, "that this is very far from the best of
all possible worlds. That's why my Jews are not all good Jews
Why should they be different from anybody else?"

Certainly few of the driven souls in *The Family Moskat* con-
tribute much to society's betterment. Singer's first novel to ap-
pear in English, it sprawls through the years 1911 to 1939 and
three generations of Warsaw's brawling, disoriented Jews. Here
(and occasionally elsewhere) he borrows several characters and
expands incidents from the fiction of Joshua Singer, whom he
credits with having taught him much of the writer's craft. But
then both draw from the same fund of people and memories;
both also utilize Gogol's sharp, kaleidoscopic detail and Flau-
bert's disciplined detachment to cut deeply into Jewish life.

The bleakness and nihilism so characteristic of European literature before World War II frame the painful encounter of traditional Judaism and twentieth century. A disorderly array of new
Jewish bohemians here mire themselves in emotional misdeeds

11

and misjudgments just when Eastern Jewry is losing its social and religious coherence and Hasidism its wholeness and joy. They reveal little of the humanity, courage, or spirituality of the ghetto fighters in John Hersey's *The Wall*, published the same year. Nor are they the familiar Jewish stereotypes isolated in an alien setting. Torn between reason and flesh, Orthodoxy and secularism, they form a vigorous, clamoring community hungry for good food, sex, wealth, and learning. Not for Singer are the pallid nuances of so much modern psychological fiction. Old and young struggle for moral perspective in a world shattered not only by war but by exposure to Western ideology and culture. With mounting uncertainty and disillusionment, Orthodox Hasidim bitterly debate Zionists, socialists, cosmopolites, and an increasingly aggressive middle class. Oblivious to the forthcoming catastrophe, all dissipate their energies in internecine quarrels, succeeding only in losing God without winning the world. Relying little upon introspection, less upon nostalgia or pathos, Singer keeps his people moving and talking.

Wealthy, stubborn, patriarchal Reb Meshulam Moskat dominates the early chapters and the small army of heirs waiting impatiently as he lives on into his eighties. Linked to their discarded pieties by social and emotional ties, the Moskats are denied full participation in Polish life not only by laws and prejudices but by their own religious taboos, intrigues, and delusions. In Singer's world few receive what they expect. When finally Reb Meshulam dies, the Moskats experience not quick riches but rapid disintegration of individual and family life. Most would agree with Heine's wry comment that Judaism is less a religion than a misfortune.

Exemplifying not only the Moskats' moral and spiritual decay but that of all Poland's Jewry is Asa Heshel Bannet, who has married into the clan. Asa Heshel has impossible dreams, a disbelief in God or man, and a flair for failure and running away. A descendant of Hasidic rabbis, he rejects Orthodoxy for Spinoza while striving for a university degree, divine truth, and earthly happiness. He attains only an obsessive cynicism and a determination to shield his individuality — by running from problems, family, and self. His talent for failure is matched only by his knack for survival. Asa Heshel survives war, prison, hunger, typhoid, and pogroms. But in a final act compounded equally of inertia, courage, and surrender, he rejects escape from Warsaw and rejoins family and friends to await the Nazis. In thus accepting death he again overcomes it. He proves one more avatar of that pervasive historical symbol the Wandering Jew — that introverted, rootless intellectual fated never to reach those whom he loves or who love him.

Singer makes it clear that philosophical abstractions mean little when confronted by physical deprivation and brutality. He rejects, with existential finality, all formulas and panaceas — including Zionism, Marxism, material wealth, religious orthodoxy, and romantic love; he emphasizes instead man's essentially tragic fate. No better life or Messiah exists. As Hitler's legions approach, Hertz Yanover, Asa Heshel's philosopher-friend, declares: "The Messiah will come soon. . . . Death is the Messiah. That's the real truth." So those who rely upon the world's philosophies to reject or soften death's inevitability are deluded. Those who preach such philosophies are innocents or frauds. Self-delusion is for Singer a cardinal sin.

Many have misread *The Family Moskat* as a bitter indictment of Poland's prewar Jews. Singer omits none of their flaws, tragic or pathetic; on the other hand, he unfailingly endows his embattled spirits with compensatory flashes of generosity and courage. Failing to win our admiration, they evoke compassion and understanding. At their worst they contain those biological juices which nourished their ancestors down the dark centuries. No outraged prophet, Singer avoids commentary or opinion and depends on "facts," forcing the reader to pass judgment. Seeing no solutions to man's dilemmas, he offers none, advising his fellow writers to do the same. What the writer considers profound and new, he has stated, is likely to be for the reader "already self-understood and banal." He thus differs sharply from novelists like Sartre and Camus, whose thinly disguised parables dramatize ideas expressed more explicitly in essay form.

The Family Moskat represents one of Singer's two major fictional modes. Like *The Magician of Lublin, The Slave,* and *The Manor,* it is essentially direct, realistic narrative. But Singer's earliest novel, *Satan in Goray,* and many of his short tales embody the demonic and supernatural. Realism and fantasy are not for Singer mutually exclusive categories but only, as he puts it, "two sides of the same coin. The world can be looked at one way or another, and the theme of a story determines its style." Whereas *The Family Moskat* has been undervalued, *Satan in Goray* has been overpraised. Written in 1932, the latter launched its twenty-eight-year-old author's "black-mirror" concern with Satan. A miracle-and-cabala narrative indebted to Yiddish gothics like S. Ansky's *The Dybbuk* and H. Leivick's *The Golem, Satan in Goray* is less novel than loosely linked vignettes. Singer here probes deeply the Jewish Messianic dream and the moral gap between the ideal and real. Borrowing from history, he chronicles the spiritual annihilation of a seventeenth-century community by the followers of a false Messiah. Viewing man's nature even more darkly than in the Moskat saga, he emphasizes that to expect on earth purity without corruption, the sacred without the profane, is sheer delusion.

From the chaos produced by the 1648 Cossack pogroms emerged a curious Messianic pretender named Sabbatai Zevi. Igniting Europe's exhausted Jews with promises of spiritual peace and earthly pleasures, he delivered only disunity and suffering. Convinced by wandering Sabbatian cultists of the Messiah's imminent arrival, entire communities abandoned not only Mosaic law but social decorum. Singer begins with Goray's isolated survivors excitedly receiving the year 1665–66; cabalist calculations have marked it as presaging the Messiah's return and the exile's termination. But Satan, not the Messiah, now appears to transform the community into a hotbed of gossip, vice, and expediency. His agents are newly arrived Sabbatians carrying word of their master's miracles and his boast to overthrow the Turkish Sultan. Disorders erupt in the prayer house as cultists and Orthodox struggle for control. Gaining the upper hand, the Sabbatians reject rabbinic law; the Messiah's arrival, they insist, invalidates the Commandments.

Goray prospers and excitement is high. But days pass without a miracle. Enthusiasm gives way to panic, shame, and bitterness; the exile of centuries is not over. Then shattering news: faced with martyrdom or conversion, Sabbatai Zevi has led a multitude into apostasy. The Sabbatian movement is shattered. The sacred have defeated the profane. Yet the victory is at best temporary and limited — with human vision and wisdom again revealed as flawed. An unnamed cabalist underscores this by summarizing briefly for posterity the entire tale — in Yiddish rather than Hebrew. (Tradition stipulates only the vernacular be used for themes of profanation.) For Singer, then, man is at once the noblest and most vulnerable of creatures. Any claim of having penetrated life's dark complexities, of having distinguished between reality and illusion or good and evil, marks one as fraud or fool. True wisdom lies in recognition of personal weakness, acceptance of sin, and patience. Goray's Jews, in their folly, would have hurried the Messiah to end their worldly pains. They learn instead they can hasten the Messiah only by curbing their own appetites — and at that the only certain Messiah is, again, death.

In this book Singer reveals virtuosity as a Yiddish stylist, employing the archaic Hebraic Yiddish of the Hebrew *pinkassim* (community chronicles). Jacob Sloan's English translation must inevitably fall short of the original, yet it does convey Singer's verbal dexterity. But despite such obvious artistry, and a deft blend of the historic, demonic, and psychological, *Satan in Goray* is one of Singer's rare aesthetic failures. Reducing his narrative to its most suggestive essentials, he allows economy to become sketchiness and overlooks some surprisingly loose ends. The insertion of demons into Goray's harshly realistic setting is so sudden and late that it jars. As events wax fantastic and abstract, Singer relies for credibility on cultural and theological details; these remain more veneer than essential. The central characters prove merely striking caricatures; only externally visible, they reveal little consistency. Several who throughout seem ignobly motivated suddenly reverse themselves. Singer here may intend irony. But without a glimpse into the protagonists' inner thoughts the reader can only feel cheated. Other characters simply are dropped. Thus much intended irony and subtlety culminate in confusion rather than coherence.

Still no other modern writer mirrors so clearly man's urge toward the sacred and yielding to the profane. Singer has read not only Freud but such Freudian precursors as Spinoza and Schopenhauer, as well as Dostoevski, who formulated for literature man's "satanic" aspects. But Singer's judgments are implicit rather than explicit, and his stories are not so much "morality tales," he insists, as narratives "constructed around a moral point of view." Whether good or evil wins out depends in his fiction on individual character as much as on events beyond human control. His refusal to condemn evil directly troubles those who miss or misread his moral concern.

A religious man rather than observant Jew, Singer believes in God, "but not in man insofar as he claims God has revealed Himself to him." He shuns organized prayer for the more personal form, rejecting dogmas as man's handiwork. Man has free choice to believe or doubt; Singer chooses to believe, describing his credo as "a sort of kasha of mysticism, deism, and skepticism," composed as it is of near-equal parts Schopenhauer, Spinoza, and the cabalist Isaac Luria. He is convinced God is with man always and everywhere, "except, perhaps, at the meetings of Marxists and other left-wingers. There is no God there; they have passed a motion to that effect." God's presence, however, is no guarantee of His intervention. A more certain intruder is Satan or one of his myriad agents, who prevent life from being neutral by forcing man to do either right or wrong. Blessed with an imagination given to sacred visions and profane apparitions, Singer draws occasionally upon Jewish mystic lore for angels but more frequently for demons, imps, and spirits. Sporting names like Samael, Asmodeus, Ketev Mriri, and Lilith, they serve as a "compositional shorthand" or "spiritual stenography" — enabling Singer to embody quickly his conviction that the thinnest line separates truth from appearance, the supernatural from the natural, virtue from sin. "I am possessed by my demons," he declares, "and they add a lot to my vision and my expression." Another world exists just beyond ours, he tells interviewers, a world not so much different from this one as its extension, projection, or mirror image. Anything is possible, therefore, in a world that may be imaginary and without substance. Certainly reason is woefully inadequate; merely passion's agent, it is incapable of extending beyond the here and now to the future and unseen. (He invites *Forward* readers to submit to him their experiences with psychic phenomena but dismisses most psychic practitioners as liars and charlatans. Still, he finds "their lies interesting. If nothing else, they are revealing fantasies.")

Singer gave shape to his views in *Gimpel the Fool and Other Stories*. These are eleven compassionate fables of Jews who otherwise interest no one but God, the devil, and themselves. God's concern is never certain. When He does make a belated appearance, He punishes not Satan, who is merely plying his trade, but a sinfully weak human. Satan and his imps move unimpeded through Polish forest, swamps, and *shtetl*, debauching the vulnerable. The *shtetl*, with its muddy streets, shabby houses, and cluttered prayer house, was at the core of East Europe's Jewish life. It has proved modern Yiddish literature's dominant image and symbol. Rabbis, scholars, and students steeped in Talmud were its important men; newspapers, radios, and automobiles were nonexistent there. Shattered by Western thought, its very traces obliterated, the *shtetl* is removed just enough in time and space to render plausible the most mythical events or legendary figures; it also is close enough to embody reality. The real and unreal fuse there convincingly. Far from romanticizing the *shtetl*, Singer presents its peculiar beauty and shabbiness, its spirituality and vulgarity. Few have seen it more clearly, felt it more intensely, expressed it more tellingly. *Shtetl* life, he emphasizes, offered compensations as well as hardships. Confronted repeatedly by hostility and uncertainty, it imposed law and decorum upon its cohesive, intimate, vulnerable community. Group and family came first. The individual was not ignored, but neither was he exalted. Forced to subordinate his idiosyncrasies to the communal pattern, he had to derive his joys from within.

In a society so firmly stable, subtle human relationships can be exposed with a precision impossible in more turbulent contexts. As a novelist of manners Singer ranks with Jane Austen, Henry

James, and Edith Wharton. But his tales transcend the regional and parochial to explore men's moral fiber under testing circumstances and their varied stratagems as they withstand or succumb to temptation. Most sorely tried here is Gimpel of Frampol, the town baker and recognized "fool." A lineal descendant of such famed "sainted fools" as Yoshe Kalb and Bontsha Schweig, Gimpel willingly accepts every jibe and cruel prank; he believes everything, even that which common sense rejects. Why? Well, after all, he reasons, anything is possible. Further, to accuse another of falsehood is to diminish his dignity. So when all Frampol conspires to marry him to Elka, the coarse-mouthed village slut, he agrees. When he becomes a father four months after becoming a husband, he accepts the child as "premature." Finding a man in his wife's bed, he views his discovery as a "hallucination" — such things do happen. His neighbors mock his gullibility, but Gimpel stands fast. Neither mistreatment nor trickery sours him. When his wife dies, Gimpel takes to the road. In his wanderings he hears many lies and falsehoods, yet he realizes there are no lies. "Whatever doesn't really happen," he declares, "is dreamed at night. It happens to one if it doesn't happen to another, tomorrow if not today, or a century hence if not next year." The physical world is for Gimpel but illusion and "once removed from the true world."

Thus Gimpel too joins the parade of Wandering Jews whose very lives testify that man's basic encounter is not between himself and God or Satan, but between self-discipline and inner needs. In this encounter Gimpel emerges triumphant. He is more fortunate, therefore, than most of the harassed little people in the collection's other tales. Satan's legions are everywhere, waiting to pounce at first hint of frailty or slackened obedience to God. Like Dostoevski, Singer often directs reader sympathy toward the narrator-as-victim. But his narrators frequently are demons or imps. An unwary reader may find himself pulling for a charmingly adroit demon to snare his weak human prey. In "From the Diary of One Not Born," for instance, the demonic narrator's pleasure proves contagious as he reduces a proud man to begging, drives an honest woman to suicide, and returns to hell for a hero's welcome. But Satan's pride in seducing the best individuals does not compare to his joy at corrupting an entire community. In "The Gentleman from Cracow," Frampol's brow-beaten Jews (who derived such pleasure from abusing Gimpel) are victimized more easily by Satan than were their Goray neighbors. Satan arrives in Frampol during a famine as a handsome young doctor and scatters gold among the starving. The growing lust for money gives way to baser desires, and the town bursts into flame. A new village rises from the ashes, but the shame lingers through generations. Frampol's later inhabitants remain paupers. A tradesman who dares ask too high a price is instructed: "Go to the gentleman from Cracow and he will give you buckets of gold."

Crushing loss causes some to become obsessed with death; others refuse to relax their grip on life, finding happiness is possible even in this the grimmest of worlds. Still no man should expect God to bestow arbitrarily so rare a gift. In "Joy," Singer makes it clear man first must be cleansed of arrogance by doubt and suffering. Rabbi Bainish's suffering approaches that of Job, but he lacks the Patriarch's unwavering faith. He curses God and deprecates creation: "There is no justice, no Judge," he cries. The world is not ruled. "A total lie! . . . In the beginning was the dung." Nothing exists beyond the moment. The rabbi may reject God's existence, but he does not doubt that of the poor. To them he gives his possessions. Nor does he, strangely enough, cease prayers, studies, or fasts. With God deed is more important than word; so despite his heresies, the rabbi has earned his reward. His dead daughter appears in a dream to declare he is soon to be summoned. This sign of heaven's concern renews the rabbi's faith, reveals to him, finally, an inscrutable God's purpose, and enables him to voice the theme underlying all eleven tales. "Life means free choice, and freedom is Mystery." Man's greatest blessing, he decides, is that God forever hides His face. The wicked make this an excuse for denial and wickedness. But for the faithful the danger is small. "If the pious man loses his faith, the truth is shown to him, and he is recalled." So, concludes Rabbi Bainish, one has cause always to be joyous.

One who would seem to have much cause for joy is Yasha Mazur, the ingratiating, scapegrace hero of *The Magician of Lublin* (1960). Yasha savors all late nineteenth-century Polish life has to offer — fame, excitement, good food, and willing women. But he is a driving, restless being who does not satisfy easily; his devoted wife and comfortable Lublin home pall early. His social masks of confidence and sophistication are paper thin. Jew and magician, he feels doubly the outsider. To fend off self-doubt and melancholy, he seeks untiringly new tricks and acrobatic stunts, possessions and mistresses. A complex maze of religious impulses and dark fantasies, good intentions and erotic entanglements, Yasha can neither stop sinning nor shrug off guilt.

On his seasonal trek from Lublin to Warsaw, Yasha unfailingly hobnobs with a group of unsavory Jewish criminals who might have stepped from the pages of Sholem Asch or Joseph Opatoshu. Awaiting him in Warsaw is the cultivated widow of a celebrated Polish university professor; she expects him to convert to Catholicism and elope with her to Italy. The move requires money, with robbery seemingly the obvious solution. But Yasha is reluctant. Despite his philandering he is proud of his honesty and his pious forebears. His halfhearted attempt at burglary goes awry, and Yasha escapes capture only by fleeing to a synagogue. There he gazes at the Ten Commandments, realizing he has broken, or planned to break, each one. His misfortunes continue. When his loyal servant-mistress, having sensed his planned elopement, hangs herself, he surrenders to guilt, remorse, and fear. The implacable inner demons he has for years repelled by will and cunning have won.

Yasha's "punishment" forms the epilogue. Three years have passed. A broken Yasha has imprisoned himself in a doorless brick cell outside his Lublin home. There he lives out his days punishing the flesh, reading holy books, and striving to regain a childhood faith in a God who sees and hears, pities and forgives. After years of self-indulgence, however, faith does not come easily. Even solitude is denied him. Word of Yasha the Penitent has spread through Poland, and the ill and unhappy flock to his barred window for advice or promise of intercession with God. When he explains he is no miracle rabbi but merely a repentant sinner, many pound, shriek, and curse their angry frustrations. Others offer bribes, flattery, or insults.

More deadly than external threats is the evil lurking in his own brain and heart. Yasha's redemption, after all, is more an act of human will than divine grace. He continues to lust, question, and doubt. But unceasing battle is as much as he, or any man, can expect. The Creator is not to be bought off; life's meaning, Yasha discovers, lies in freedom and therefore discipline. As for atonement and absolution, these come not from God but from one's victims. So peace will elude Yasha until his final breath. His single consolation is that God, being merciful and compassionate, will assure good's ultimate triumph in the next world.

Yasha is as much Western picaro as Yiddish folk hero. Rarely do Yiddish characters make what Irving Howe terms the Aristotelian "climb from *hybris* into humility." Most have little occasion for "pride." Yiddish writers traditionally have rejected

worldly standards of greatness as mere expressions of physical ap-
petite; they have focused instead upon the unheroic who "live
and endure in silence" and whose endings lack dramatic climax
or social impact. On the other hand, Yasha's hybris is alloyed always by a Yiddish awe of God and fear of inner drives and ambi-
tions. But his world is broader than that of Mendele's Fishke or
Sholom Aleichem's Tevye or Mottel, who are confined within
Jewish boundaries. Yasha moves convincingly into the non-Jewish world and back. Singer thereby introduces a theme long pop-
ular among American-Jewish novelists: the love of their Jewish
heroes for Gentile women, who symbolize not only sexual taboo
but a world of social gentility too foreign to be entered success-
fully.

That *The Magician of Lublin* does not involve the reader as
deeply and movingly as does *Gimpel the Fool and Other Stories*
is hardly grounds for complaint. The novel's spare, sinewy language conveys effectively the familiar Singerian world wherein a
distant God chooses not to interfere in man's eternal struggle
with the dark powers. Here man's greatest fears need be not of
others but of himself. He cannot for a moment indulge his inner
cravings; within the hidden corners of his being demons of perversity and desire struggle for his soul by blocking him from self-
discipline and compassion for others. No middle road exists: the
single step from God plunges man into a moral abyss.

The Magician of Lublin evoked complaint from several critics
that Singer overemphasizes the sexual; so strong a concern for
the erotic, they have contended, is contrary to Yiddish tradition.
But a reading of earlier Yiddish fiction reveals a persistent regard
for the flesh. (A similar charge was leveled a generation earlier at
Sholem Asch.) Still, the objection merits attention. Certainly
Singer's desire to titillate is undeniable. "In my stories," he has
stated, "it is just one step from the study house to sexuality and

back again. Both phases of human existence have continued to interest me." His handling of the erotic, however, is the most effective in a Yiddish context since Asch's *God of Vengeance* or Zalman Schneour's *Jews of Shklov*. Singer's earthiness rings true. Fed on centuries of poverty and fear, East Europe's Jews had little use for asceticism or the Christian suspicion of the flesh. Recurrent pogroms made urgent the Biblical dictum to be fruitful and multiply.

Singer neither champions nor condemns man's physical cravings. He simply makes it clear that his Jews (especially the Hasidim, who stress joy, song, and dance) retain enough vigor after life's demands to satisfy fleshly yearnings — despite beard, earlock, or matron's wig. Never condoning license, he points repeatedly to the dangers implicit in excessive yielding to passion. Such excess is socially and emotionally dangerous, rendering man vulnerable and punishment inevitable. Singer has derived much of his earthy, colloquial immediacy from the Hasidic folktales. (Martin Buber's twice-told, "antiseptic" anecdotes are not for him.) Moving in and out of the realistic tradition, his tales take on a timeless quality. Their Jewish ceremony and folklore provide a framework for all humanity's dreams and desires. Dates are occasional and irrelevant; the action frequently could be shifted backward or forward without affecting character or setting. Wandering through ghetto and countryside, often denied the simple dignity of citizenship, their feverish little people feel themselves outside history; the world's calendar and events do not reach them. A day's passing means only Messiah and redemption are that much closer. Not one is a symbolic abstraction. Lusty, insatiable, and absurdly human, they struggle briefly, frantically; then, bewildered and exhausted, they succumb. The lowest chimney sweeps, beggars, thieves, and prostitutes have a dignity no disaster can destroy.

Neither prophet nor reformer, Singer lays bare, without shock or outrage, the intensity of their struggles. More existential and modern than many writers dealing with today's familiar materials, he rejects convenient platitudes of alienation, loneliness, or defeat. No character is permitted to rely upon God alone for spiritual victory. God is no mere protector; He gives, as Yasha Mazur discovered, few hints of what is permitted or forbidden. Never denying God's existence, Singer's skeptics (often Spinoza disciples) insist only that no man knows the truth of His divine being. So he who expects a universe of pure justice and reason, of virtue without evil, is a fool. In Singer (as in much Yiddish fiction — and Shakespeare) only for the saintly innocent is there hope. A Gimpel, Yoshe Kalb, Bontsha Schweig, or Lear's fool expects so little from life that his total acceptance of deprivation and suffering becomes a protective shield denied the more worldly or wise.

Singer distinguishes between the true pietists (rabbis primarily) and those pious pretenders (cabalists frequently) who corrupt their learning for material ends. Still he has no quarrel with cabalist or other ideas sincerely held and moderately espoused. Common sense, discipline, occasionally learning, and always luck are needed to avoid personal disaster. Calamity may result from the lack of any one. If compassion is missing, for instance, piety, asceticism, and intellectualism are useless. Even his pietists recognize worldly rewards are more likely for the strong or lucky than the weak or unlucky, but for no one is reward certain.

Testing these truths is the bizarre array of merchants and beggars, scholars and prostitutes who enact the eleven tales compiled in *The Spinoza of Market Street* (1961). These discover quickly that they are their own worst enemies and that the merest misstep means loss of paradise. Most confuse the paths to heaven and hell in revealing, as one critic puts it, Singer's "infinitely tender and infinitely ruthless meditations on the human condition."

They also prove Singer's imaginative powers are not inexhaustible. Here his familiar mixture of folklore, religion, and legend does not win that easy suspension of disbelief so vital in tales of fantasy. Formula too often replaces insight as characters and plots seem pale recastings of various *Goray* characters and *Gimpel* tales. Yet even second-level Singer is of a quality higher than that attained by most writers today. And each tale does test anew the eternal tensions between reason and emotion, denial and license. The title story, for instance, underlines again the folly of denying the flesh. Above Warsaw's bustling Market Street, Dr. Nahum Fischelson, a lonely old scholar, spends his nights contemplating the heavens and his days writing a commentary on Spinoza's *Ethics*. For this task he has neglected ambition, comfort, and feelings. He views disdainfully those in the noisy street below who do pursue such things. They satisfy not reason but their intoxicated emotions.

When World War I halts Fischelson's meager pension he is saved from starvation by Black Dobbe, an ugly, hard-bitten peddler whose street battles leave little time for the metaphysical. She plies Fischelson with food and attention; to his surprise, he discovers a joy in living. To his further amazement, he finds himself in a marital bed. Frightened by the corporeal, Fischelson protests to his blushing bride that he has promised nothing; he is an old man and weak. Black Dobbe has not waited these many years to be fed dialectic on her marriage night; she silently embraces her trembling philosopher, who finally drops Spinoza's *Ethics* to the floor and consummates their union. Later Fischelson is guilt-ridden at having betrayed Spinoza by succumbing to bodily passion. He gazes skyward to declare: "Divine Spinoza, forgive me. I have become a fool." But the old man's real foolishness lies in failing to recognize his first act of true wisdom. Ignorance, Singer makes clear, lies in denying the essential unity of flesh and spirit.

Those who refuse to accept this basic truth, or to fulfill their mortal obligations, pay for such arrogance even after death. The line between this life and the next is too thin to offer escape. Thus neither life nor death guarantees peace. Yet in "The Beggar Said So" Singer does suggest that simple, unquestioning faith may make life meaningful and post-mortal serenity a possibility. Some, however, reject belief and kindness for lie and trick. These prove Satan's special delight. He enjoys nothing more, he explains in "A Tale of Two Liars," than the clever thief with a knack for self-destruction. He then describes how a pair of magnificent con artists destroy each other. Most humans, however, are neither very evil nor virtuous, merely weak or unlucky. Chance largely determines their fates, with the difference between fortune and disaster being small indeed. An accident, a momentary miscalculation or weakness alters their lives. The fortunate, several tales here make clear, have nothing to crow about but their undeserved good luck. The unlucky have the poorhouse, or worse.

One who has it much worse is Hindele, in "The Black Wedding," in whom family melancholy and eccentricities have given way to madness. She dies convinced she has succumbed to Satan. Real or imagined, Hindele's demons have won. Satan relishes his every conquest, even over so pitiful a victim as Hindele. But in "The Destruction of Kreschev" he can boast again of vanquishing not only an innocent bride but an entire community. He chooses his targets well. So squalid and barren is Kreschev that there God Himself "dozes among the clouds." After all, gloats Satan, "the Almighty is old; it is no easy task to live forever." So Satan indulges there his love of mismating the old and young, beautiful and ugly, good and corrupt. There he causes the innocent Lise to forsake "both this world and next between the saying of a 'yes' and a 'no.'" He has made his point: so interwoven are

27

love and hate, mercy and cruelty, joy and pain that values are easily confused and perverted. With the world distorted, the soul can only be lost.

Natural order is reversed completely in the nether world of "Shiddah and Kuziba." Here light is evil, black is virtue, and Satan is the Creator. The she-devil Shiddah and her son Kuziba flee in terror at the approach of light, which betokens man — that God-mistaken "mixture of flesh, love, dung, and lust." Shiddah's worst fears are realized when her underground haven crumbles beneath heavy drills. Workmen enter amid glaring light, and mother and son retreat toward earth's hated surface. They will hide there in marshes and graves while awaiting that final dark victory when God and Satan become one. Man will then have proved a bad dream, a minor distraction in God's eternal life.

God does occasionally have the last word. Even so, He first extends man's patience and loyalty before displacing Satan to reveal His own holy plan. In *The Slave* (1962), Singer's best novel, Satan's final victory repeatedly seems imminent. Returning to the infamous Chmielnicki massacres, Singer drops both his chatty tale-spinner and malicious demon-narrator; he tells instead an old-fashioned tale of devoted lovers who withstand crushing societal pressures to achieve what Susan Sontag terms a "tearfully satisfying" reunion-in-death. Jacob of Josefov has learned early that to expect more joy than suffering is to deny reality. Jacob's sufferings enable Singer to explore the complexities of freedom and slavery, sin and redemption. Blending elements from the Biblical legends of Jacob, Job, and Ruth, he underscores man's tenacity and courage in terms that are by turn earthy and idyllic, compassionate and cruel. Jacob has lost wife and children to Cossack pogroms which decimated his village. Captured by brigands, he has been sold to a Polish farmer in a remote mountain village. Left alone to tend cattle for months at a time, he struggles to retain a Jewish identity. Self-discipline comes hard at twenty-nine, especially when eager peasant girls and carousing villagers offer temptation. He need only pretend to convert to be free, but God is watching.

Jacob's greatest temptation is Wanda Bzik, his master's beautiful daughter, who repeatedly saves his life. Jacob resists seduction for four hard years. But, like all Singer heroes, he learns that ultimately the flesh is not to be denied. Despite a crushing sense of guilt and eventual tragedy, he capitulates to Wanda. Before making love to her he insists she take an icy bath and immediately afterward declare herself a daughter of Israel. Their union violates Polish, as well as Jewish, law. Discovery means certain death. Still Jacob experiences his first happiness. Finally ransomed, Jacob returns for Wanda. She converts to Judaism, takes the matriarchal name of Sarah, and joins Jacob in a life of fearful wandering to escape detection. Their subsequent life together is filled with uncertainty and disappointment, with Wanda-Sarah playing mute to disguise her Gentile origin. Jacob retains his faith through it all. Like Yasha Mazur, Jacob learns man must accept the world as God has decreed it, that God's law and purpose require man to choose daily between good and evil. Such free choice, it is clear, cannot function without evil, nor can mercy exist without sorrow. No formulas will suffice. In time Sarah is exposed, dies in childbirth, and is buried in unsanctified ground. Jacob is arrested, escapes, and with his son begins an arduous trip to the Holy Land. He sadly considers how his life parallels that of the Patriarch Jacob. The ancient laws and griefs, he sighs, remain the same.

Twenty years later a white-bearded Jacob returns from Jerusalem to Pilitz, where Sarah is buried. With age has come the belief that everything God does is good, including His intermingling of sacred and profane, beautiful and ugly: "An eye was watching, a hand guiding, each sin had its significance." Jacob's story has grown into legend, and his return causes great excitement. But he dies without finding Sarah's unmarked plot. Yet God *has* been watching. The gravedigger shoveling out Jacob's grave uncovers a still recognizable Sarah. Pilitz's astounded inhabitants are convinced only a saint's body could have withstood two decades of worms and elements. God has proclaimed the lovers' innocence for all to see.

The Slave finds Singer at his most effective. Nowhere does he express so movingly man's undying concern for the spirit and unfailing surrender to the flesh. No reward, he again makes clear, should be expected on earth. Yet all need not despair, for there are those for whom even the most crushing defeats may serve as a means of exploring and elevating the human spirit. True holiness and love transcend time and tragedy, cruelty and injustice, to attain a higher, heavenly reward. Indeed, those few who — like Gimpel, Yasha Mazur, Jacob and Sarah — accept not only suffering's inevitability but its necessity attain a measure of serenity on earth. But such beings are rare. Singer's prose, always spare and controlled, is here lyrical, his imagery precise. He reveals again his flair for sustaining interest and concern in the bizarre and remote. And rare in Yiddish fiction is his easy blending of plot, structure, and physical nature.

Short Friday (1964), however, is not of like quality. It consists of sixteen standard, rather than vintage, Singer tales of the Lublin district. Several reveal an element of strain, of a craftsman struggling with his craft — or perhaps not struggling enough and writing from formula rather than excited imagination. Singer has repeatedly expressed his belief in demonic spirits — at least as accurate symbols of human behavior. *Short Friday* validates his claim while pointing up its danger. His devils and imps sometimes prove overly facile devices evoked — without adequate logic, motivation, or avoidance of repetition — to enliven a thin plot. Singer tries to extend his imagination farther than in the past, to stretch his special vision to include such acts of desperation as murder, animalism, and lesbianism. "Never fear the sensational, the perverse, the pathological, the mystical," he has stated. "Life has no exceptions." He seemingly sets out to prove this. Yet if no tale here is quite another "Gimpel the Fool," none is without Singer's special flair and flavor. Each is peopled by his slightly grotesque *shtetl* types whose exotic speech, dress, and habits somehow encompass humanity's joys and dreams, sufferings and sins.

Concerned as always with the dark inner struggles between man's angels and demons, Singer is equally involved with those battles waged more openly and crudely by husbands, wives, and lovers. These too expose good and evil's interlocking unity and remind us that in the God-man dialogue God often remains silent and inscrutable. They remind us also that man's path is precarious in a world torn between God and Satan. One misstep, indulgence, breach of faith gives Satan's watchful legions their opening. "Blood," the volume's shocker, underscores this vividly in tracing the frantic degeneration of the sensual young Risha, who betrays her enfeebled husband with an unscrupulous ritual slaughterer. The two soon find sexual satisfaction only amid the warmly flowing blood of animals they have butchered. Such carnality would not have surprised the ancient cabalists; their sages had insisted "the passion for blood and the passion for flesh have the same origin." They had known also that "one transgression begets another." Risha slides from adultery and bloodletting to blasphemy, apostasy, and madness — until chased and killed as a werewolf. Stretching credibility, yet steering clear of fantasy, Singer anchors Risha's outlandish behavior in realistic detail and insight. Extending Singer's skill and judgment even farther is

"Yentl the Yeshiva Boy," wherein he mixes quaintly the religious and erotic, lesbianism and homosexuality. Against a backdrop of student life, study, and talk, Singer unfolds a perverse comedy of a girl whose gender seems a mistake.

Yet mistakes are likely anywhere. That mortals sin is hardly surprise enough to raise eyebrows in heaven. But angels giving vent to evil impulses cause a stir on high. "Jachid and Jechidah" presents a Platonic heaven where souls exist before birth and man's world is a Miltonic hell for fallen spirits (with all humans viewed as heaven's rejects). Singer alters his angle of vision to present truth as relative — a matter of ironic perspective. He also reverses the life-death cycle — all this by means of a pair of freethinking angels (or "souls") who hold the blasphemous opinion spirits are not created but evolve. They even reject free will and ultimate good and evil. For their crimes the two are sentenced to death — this means earth, with its "horrors called flesh, blood, marrow, nerves, and breath." Singer thus frames a second philosophical essay in slight, but exotic, fictional terms. ("Shiddah and Kuziba" had conveyed a demon's-eye view of earth and hell.) His effort proves imaginative and intriguing enough to override the strained imagery and unexpectedly preachy overtones. More substantial as narrative are two of his earliest forays into American life, "Alone" and "A Wedding in Brownsville." Here Miami and Brooklyn spawn events as nightmarish and demonic as any in Frampol or Lublin, events that force their confused protagonists to meditate on what lies behind appearance and reality and to recall the Nazi holocaust.

Even more biting than "Alone" and "A Wedding in Brownsville," however, is the wryly humorous "The Last Demon," whose verve and witty horror make it *Short Friday*'s most memorable tale. Here too past, present, and holocaust merge. The demon-narrator's insulated world consists solely of Jews and demons —

no outsiders allowed. "I don't have to tell you," he declares, "that I am a Jew. What else, a Gentile? I've heard that there are Gentile demons, but I don't know any, nor do I wish to know them." Assigned to the "God-forsaken village" of Tishevitz to corrupt a pious young rabbi, he is defeated on the verge of victory. His failure dooms him to remain in Tishevitz for "eternity plus a Wednesday." Thanks to the Nazis, eternity proves shorter than expected and man crueler than any devil. Our narrator is not surprised; most demons find man terrifying. No true devil, he laments, could have conceived the Nazis' grandiose cruelty. Indeed, for mere demons the devout and learned (like the young rabbi) always have been tough adversaries — but pathetically easy victims for Hitler's troopers. These last have obliterated Jewish Poland, Tishevitz included, with its demon world. A lone survivor, the narrator is being forced into retirement. "Why demons," he asks, "when man himself is a demon?" Still he is a Jewish devil and shares the Jewish sorrow. "There are no more Jews, no more demons. . . . We have also been annihilated," he cries. "I am the last, a refugee."

No gory detail shows as Singer again mourns the holocaust's victims. He also departs from his rule of offering "neither judge, nor judgment" in his tales. He here speaks, albeit indirectly, to charges leveled by his more caustic critics — some of whom view him as Yiddish literature's "last demon." If things were not bad enough, his narrator laments wryly, he and his fellow demons are being displaced as corrupters of Jews — by Yiddish writers whose stories adulterate traditional beliefs and values. Jews of old fed mind, soul, and spirit on Hebrew law and alphabet; now they have only tales of "Sabbath pudding cooked in pig's fat." Even the narrator draws sustenance from a tattered Yiddish storybook. His book's words, our demon admits, not only form "gibberish" but parody Hebrew law. He is keenly aware his own behavior merely parodies that of the rabbis. Yet is not even a parody better than nothing? He shudders only at realizing that when his volume of Yiddish tales goes, so does he. "When the last letter is gone,/ The last of the demons is done." His critics, Singer seems to imply, might give thought to this grim eventuality.

Aging survivors and fading memories trace the Jewish world Singer remembers. Writing *as if* this world still lives, he rejects the charge that his literary stance is artificial. "After all," he asks, "what could be more artificial than marriage? . . . Every man assumes he will go on living. He behaves *as if* he will never die. . . . It's very natural and healthy. . . . We have to go on living and we have to go on writing." Time only intensifies his efforts to give his world new, enduring life by his fiction. He has tried to reactivate its ghosts and sounds in a cluster of autobiographical sketches published collectively as *In My Father's Court* (1966). A three-level memoir that fills out the Singer family portrait outlined earlier in Joshua Singer's *Of a World That Is No More* (1946, Yiddish), these recollections reveal the deep human well from which both Singers have drawn their fiction. For the family of Rabbi Pinchos Menachem Singer life in the Warsaw ghetto a half-century ago was hardly dull. A frantic, bizarre array of butchers and bakers, drifters and tearful women, criminals and saints shuffled through their modest Krochmalna Street apartment, atop a reeking, garbage-strewn stairway. There Rabbi Singer conducted his rabbinical court, the Beth Din. Rooted in Jewish tradition, the court combined synagogue, law court, and psychoanalyst's consulting room. Isaac Singer recalls it was for him "the celestial council of justice, God's judgment . . . absolute mercy." He eavesdropped from infancy on those troubled pietists and penitents "for whom the supernatural was so real it was almost negotiable." Most acted out their foolish, desperate, or selfless lives to the Mosaic law's very letter, developing thereby a wide range of behavioral quirks and obsessions. Krochmalna Street teemed with life and energy. Evoking that life with warmth, humor, verve, and, assumedly, imagination, Singer retells some of its uncountable tales. These Krochmalna Street sketches even have a "hero": Pinchos Menachem Singer. Scholarly, shy, innocent, fearful of the world's corruptions, he obviously has served as prototype for his son's numerous rabbinical saints. "In our home, the world itself was *tref* — unclean," Singer recalls. "Many years were to pass before I began to understand how much sense there was in this attitude."

Other vignettes deal more directly with the author's own escapades and encounters. Amid intermittent impressions of journalistic haste, Singer provides rich insights into his boyhood. A significant event was a trip with his mother, during World War I, from German-occupied Warsaw to remote Bilgoray, where generations of his family had lived. His maternal grandfather had been that *shtetl*'s longtime rabbi; his uncle was the present one. Both are recognizable from his fiction. Bilgoray had changed little in several centuries. Young Isaac literally was able to enter and relive his past, to penetrate layers of Jewish customs and values. "In this world of old Jewishness I found a spiritual treasure trove. I had a chance to see our past as it really was. Time seemed to flow backwards. I lived Jewish history." For a future novelist it was a find beyond price.

These sketches also trace, almost inadvertently, the intellectual collapse of Poland's six-century-old Jewish community. People and incidents echo those to be found in *The Family Moskat* and *The Manor*, as well as in Joshua Singer's *The Brothers Ashkenazi*. For the brothers Singer these experiences shaped a psychological pattern of spiritual rebellion, temporary exile, and final return. They were far from alone. This century's first two decades found young Jews rejecting Talmud for socialism and the rabbis

35

BEN SIEGEL

for Dostoevski; many clipped their earlocks to become painters
and writers rather than yeshiva students. Among these was
Joshua Singer. To his parents' shocked dismay, he also drew
young Isaac into his world of freethinkers and artists. The latter
records his adolescent delight at visiting his brother's bohemian
friends; wandering into a sculptor's studio he discovered a daz-
zling new world where body and mind were honored as fervently
as the Orthodox reverenced soul and spirit. He was caught irretrievably.

In this feverish atmosphere the two Singers grew to manhood.
Joshua was a joiner of bohemian movements. Isaac was and is a
loner; no movement engages his deepest sympathies. In Bilgoray,
the rabbi's younger grandson caused consternation by reading
not only Yiddish secularists but such corruptive worldlings as
Strindberg, Turgenev, Tolstoi, Maupassant, Chekhov, and the
excommunicate Spinoza, whose writings created "a turmoil" in
his young brain. Isaac Singer's comment about his brother soon
was self-applicable: "he had deserted the old, but there was nothing in the new that he could call his own." Their experiences
profile a figure prominent in their fiction — the spiritual outsider
torn by the demands of mind, flesh, and spirit. A deeply felt testi-
monial to the world Hitler's crematoria reduced to ashes, *In My
Father's Court* conveys the essence of a rich Yiddish culture now
barely a memory. Singer underscores its humanity and eccentricities, its family warmth and angers, its ironbound faith and cus-
tom. When he discusses his family, his usual irony is constrained.
But in the tribute paid to Warsaw's Jews, who "lived in sanctity
and died as martyrs," his muted, moving sorrow shades into bitter, laconic eloquence.

Impatient young Jewish intellectuals, much like those of his
own Warsaw days, reappear in Singer's *The Manor* (1967). Written between 1953 and 1955, this novel is the first of a two-volume

old-style family chronicle that, like *The Family Moskat*, can double as a political-intellectual history of Eastern Europe. (The second volume, *The Estate*, has not yet been translated into English.) Rich in incident, dialogue, and description, it moves back to 1863 to follow a small cluster of Jews and Poles through the quarter-century after Russia's crushing of the Polish insurrection. Singer had thought of calling this volume "The Beginning," since it describes early socialist and Zionist stirrings in Poland. The country's social values and forms here are scrambled. Polish noblemen flee the police while Jews enjoy a rare respite of freedom and prosperity. Emerging from ghettos and *shtetls*, the latter share in the new industrialism and radicalism. Older Jews cling to Torah and prayers, watching bewilderedly as their children turn revolutionaries to redeem mankind.

Events revolve around pious Calman Jacoby and to a lesser extent the decadent Count Wladislaw Jampolski. As Calman's fortunes rise, the Count's decline; leasing the dispossessed nobleman's estate or "manor," Calman becomes wealthy. On the manor he wins and loses a world; there he watches his children grow, leave his house, and fashion their own lives. Expanding enterprises force him into non-Jewish contacts; devout and disciplined, he prays hard and eats sparingly. He also makes mistakes. Ambition, lust, pride, and family concern drive him hard. Success and pleasure, he finds, exact a price steep in weakened moral values, traditions, and family ties.

Calman's four daughters share his risks. Two marry pious Jews and slip easily into the traditional ways. Another, Miriam Lieba, is a fantasizing romantic who converts to Catholicism to plunge into a disastrous marriage with Lucian Jampolski, the Count's unstable, dissolute son. Shaindel Jacoby seemingly makes a more tenable marriage to Ezriel Babad, son of a Hasidic rabbi. But Ezriel's earlocks and black gaberdine mask a skeptic less interested in God than in science, contradictions in Holy Writ, and Voltaire, Kepler, and Newton. Such things, his father warns, lead inevitably to modern dress, loss of faith, even apostasy. Rabbi Menachem Mendel Babad (modeled closely after the author's father) proves prophetic. With the years Ezriel outgrows both his Hasidic past and his dowdy wife; he also develops strong resemblances to Yasha Mazur, Asa Heshel Bannet — and Joshua and Isaac Singer (even to living on Krochmalna Street). He finally becomes a successful neurologist, only to learn science offers no more "truth" or certainty than does religious faith. But for Ezriel's generation the old, fixed values are gone; fear of social failure or political arrest has replaced fear of God.

Missing neither group's soft spots, Singer sympathizes with both — the older generation's reluctance to relinquish the past and youth's clamor for rapid change. Calman Jacoby clearly reflects Singer's mixed feelings; Calman is as illogical as he is sincere: he cuts down a forest to provide ties for a railroad that can only accelerate the very changes he deplores. Nor is Calman's final retreat into his private synagogue any more meaningful beyond the individual level than was Yasha Mazur's into his cell. Retreat (religious or temporal) offers at best, Singer emphasizes, only the most tenuous escape. He rejects equally past dogmatism, present relativism, and the ever-popular philosophy of despair. Individual choice, action, and responsibility are what matter. Only by accepting the burden of his acts can man survive his self-created frustrations.

The Manor conveys more than it mentions. Hitler, Auschwitz, the Warsaw ghetto uprising are still far in the future. But with the new century's approach these catastrophes seem tangible and close enough to render near meaningless all this frenzied human striving. Indeed, each character's unawareness of his world's eventual fate adds poignancy. Richly textured, tightly structured, lu cidly written, *The Manor* still disappoints. Singer relies even more heavily than usual upon plot to reveal character; Aristotle might approve, but surface narrative and situation predominate at cost of motive, insight, and depth. Introspective monologues are few, brief, inconclusive. Events move in swift, chainlike sequence, with people emerging just long enough to reveal momentary inclinations. Some, like the Jampolskis, fade out unexpectedly; others reappear only at long intervals. Author and characters seem poised for the future and volume two; several figures, for instance, are introduced so late as to imply further development.

These flaws, however, merely lessen the novel's potential without weakening its eloquent, sharply realized detail or dramatic impact. Singer best sums up his intent by observing that "It is not child's play to be born, to marry, to bring forth generations, to grow old, to die. These are matters no jester's witticisms can belittle." Nor can a critic's carpings diminish them. Singer again delineates with authority and fidelity the ethos of a time and people known and imagined and now irretrievably lost. Such qualities result only when a creative imagination has utilized fully a sensitive insider's knowledge and a disciplined artist's perspective.

In *The Séance* (1968), his latest collection, Singer concentrates more on the old and dying than on babies or brides. Most of the sixteen tales are recent, several go back a few years, and one is a quarter-century old. Their characters are frenetically familiar: unworldly rabbis and scheming upstarts, good men gone foolish, bureaucratic angels and rebellious dybbuks, and several corpses who dance between life and grave. The Evil One, however, is less evident, appearing primarily to insist neither judge nor judgment exists; in fact, fewer demons generally are called upon than in the past. They are not needed — enough devilish humans are

39

available for the inevitable mischief. God? Seemingly He sits in His seventh heaven snapping His fingers at everything. Other changes or "shifts" emerge. Recent tales are longer and more dense in thought and detail. Women narrators are more frequent, as are symbolic or prophetic dreams. Most surprising is a lessening of authorial detachment. Singer's views on psychic phenomena and man's abuse of animals do not obtrude but repeatedly motivate the action. Singer makes clear, however, that man's major cruelties are reserved still for those fellow humans showing him the most kindness. And so perverse is the human animal that perpetrator and victim often reverse roles, with the victim feeling the more guilty. In "The Plagiarist," for instance, gentle Reb Kasriel Dan Kinsker cannot resist a brief, angry wish that harm befall a disciple who, after plagiarizing his manuscripts, schemes to displace him as town rabbi. When the latter falls ill and dies, the rabbi decides he has failed a divine test of his moral strength; he has broken, he declares, the Commandment not to kill. Resigning his position, he wanders off to do penance. Somewhat reminiscent of Saul Bellow's *The Victim*, "The Plagiarist" provides an evocative glance at the tangled roots of guilt and innocence.

Equally relevant to today's moral confusion is "The Slaughterer," a taut, mind-wrenching variation on "Blood," Singer's earlier probing of the psychological ties between slaughter and worship. Sensitive, scholarly Yoineh Meir has prepared to be the Kolomir rabbi, but no man, it seems, escapes this world's sorrows. Instead of rabbi, he is appointed ritual slaughterer. Constant bloodletting moved the sensual Risha (in "Blood") to deepening carnality and degeneracy; Yoineh Meir experiences revulsion, guilt, and depression. "Even in the worm that crawls in the earth," he cries, "there glows a divine spark. When you slaughter a creature, you slaughter God." Yet signs of slaughter are everywhere; not only his phylacteries and holy books are of animal skin, but the Torah itself. Insanity or death alone promises escape. Shouting God Himself is "a slaughterer . . . and the whole world . . . a slaughterhouse," Yoineh Meir plunges into madness and the river. The community has little time to grieve; a new slaughterer must be summoned for the holidays.

Yoineh Meir may find even death lacks repose. Certainly none is exhibited by the deceased in "The Dead Fiddler," a long tale of twists, turns, and wild, sad humor. Heaven and earth conspire often to hide the truth, it seems, while reality hangs by a thread and delusion overshadows all. Equally bizarre is the "love" story of "Zeitl and Rickel," two orphaned girls who, having had more than their share of sadness, form a lesbian relationship. Driven by curiosity and concern over future punishment, they seek to hurry matters by a double suicide. Singer displays his usual tact, but the wit and point of "Yentl the Yeshiva Boy," his previous literary foray into lesbianism, is lacking. More memorable than these two pitiable misfits is Wolf Ber, thief-hero of "The Brooch." A skilled safecracker and occasional pickpocket, Wolf Ber attributes success to a strict personal code. Like many another underworldling, he separates home from profession. But life does not divide so easily or neatly. His adored Celia shatters their cozy world by stealing an expensive brooch and lying about it. When he forces a confession, she turns defiant. He is a thief — why not she? No, he replies, his family cannot hold two thieves. How much, after all, is God expected to stand? "If she is a thief, I must become an honest man."

When strong, clever thieves find life crushing, what chance have honest, less adroit mortals? Certainly life on this side of the Atlantic for the aging, uncertain Jewish writers Singer lately seems fond of portraying is no less harsh than in old Poland. He adds to a growing roster of disoriented scribblers three whose misadventures in New York and Montreal exemplify his repeated conviction that all metaphysical speculations pale before fleshly needs. More positively expressed here than in earlier novels and tales, this theme enables Singer to convey his varied — and sometimes varying — views on the occult, dreams, compassion, and the deterioration of Judaica (that "vanishing specialty") in America. He continues also to confront the holocaust's residual horrors and human vestiges.

Dr. Zorach Kalisher, in "The Séance," is one such vestige. A shabby refugee scholar without prospects, he sponges meals from Lotte Kopitzky, an inept student of the occult who brings him "messages" from his dead relatives and mistress. Long grown cynical, he regards her as ridiculous and her séances as a joke but goes along with her messages and automatic writings, paintings, and symphonies. His doubts are confirmed when, after an embarrassing comedy of errors, he discovers in her bathroom the woman hired to pose as his dead mistress. Chagrined but undaunted, Lotte Kopitzky cries: "You're laughing huh? There is no death, there isn't any. We live forever, and we love forever. This is the pure truth." Singer seems to agree with the kindly old fraud, thus veering sharply from his ringing conclusion to *The Family Moskat* that "Death is the Messiah. That's the real truth." But more important than glib generalities about life, death, or truth, Singer implies, is even the feeblest attempt to reach out — as has Lotte Kopitzky — to another human being.

One who would agree with her rejection of death is Herman Gombiner, the sickly, fiftyish protagonist of "The Letter Writer," the collection's longest tale. An editor in a Hebrew publishing house on New York's Canal Street, Herman lives alone and believes himself able to see "beyond the façade of phenomena," having experienced since childhood numerous apparitions, telepathic incidents, clairvoyant visions, and prophetic dreams. Miracles are for Herman a daily occurrence; one has to be blind, he insists, not to acknowledge the concern of God or Providence for man's most trivial needs. His faith in Providence and psychic phenomena is confirmed when he contracts pneumonia and Rose Beechman, a new pen pal, appears to nurse him. Her dead grandmother, she explains, has summoned her to his side. When he recovers, these two near-strangers realize they are sharing a new miracle: neither will face old age alone. Moving and suggestive despite excessive length, "The Letter Writer" provides Singer with an excuse not only to probe the occult but to describe life in a crumbling Hebrew publishing house; his unsparing profiles of its staff members must have drawn blood and mirth along Canal Street. He also probes here (as in "The Last Demon") the writer's contribution to Jewish life and survival. In "The Lecture" (a rather incongruous *Playboy*-award winner) he does so a third time, and his conclusions are no more reassuring than before.

Half of *The Séance*'s offerings are vintage Singer, and even these might have gained from judicious editing and compression. Undoubtedly he would strike oftener to heart and marrow were he to publish less. But Singer's tales, as mentioned above, occasionally disappoint primarily because of the expectations aroused by his better work. Critics given to labels and categories apply to Singer such terms as modernist, traditionalist, gothicist, or even demonist; they like relating him to noted storytellers like Dostoevski, Tolstoi, and Dickens. Each term or link may have validity. But Singer is essentially his own man as individual and artist. His dignity, compassion, incisive intelligence, and originality are as evident as is his deep dedication to his craft. His unique vision gives to Jewish tradition, history, and lore new meaning and application.

This vision is broad as well as unique. For Singer no intellectual mode suffices alone; none proves a panacea for man's doubts and fears. Finding asceticism and indulgence equally unappeal-

43

ing, he rejects pointless sensuality, intellectualism, or parochialism for universal values of moderation and generosity or sincerity of spirit. Neither optimist nor cynic, Singer never strikes poses through his characters to defy faith or to disdain learning. He observes his struggling figures without intruding judgment or sympathy; both seem almost irrelevant, but they prove otherwise. Through every tale runs a clear line that divides good and evil and renders an implied moral verdict on every act.

Singer's intent, however, is less to criticize his bedeviled fellow beings than to understand and reveal them. Despite his meticulous depiction of setting, manner, and belief, he never allows these elements to become as important as each character's painful self-scrutiny. The historical moment also is secondary. Singer strives for those acts of revelation that catch his proud, lustful, deluded little people at points of great stress, acts that cut through the banalities of religion, culture, and setting to expose their common substance across the generations. Ultimately, their loneliness and longings, their painful awareness of self and inevitable self-doubts, constitute a penetrating inquiry not into Jewish but into universal existence.

⤴ *Selected Bibliography*

Works of Isaac Bashevis Singer

NOVELS AND COLLECTIONS OF SHORT STORIES

The Family Moskat, translated by A. H. Gross. New York: Knopf, 1950.

Satan in Goray, translated by Jacob Sloan. New York: Noonday Press, 1955.

Gimpel the Fool and Other Stories, translated by Saul Bellow, Isaac Rosenfeld, and others. New York: Noonday Press, 1957.

The Magician of Lublin, translated by Elaine Gottlieb and Joseph Singer. New York: Noonday Press, 1960.

The Spinoza of Market Street, translated by Martha Glicklich and others. New York: Farrar, Straus and Cudahy, 1961.

The Slave, translated by the author and Cecil Hemley. New York: Farrar, Straus and Cudahy, 1962.

Short Friday and Other Stories, translated by Joseph Singer, Roger Klein, and others. New York: Farrar, Straus and Giroux, 1964.

The Manor, translated by Joseph Singer and Elaine Gottlieb. New York: Farrar, Straus and Giroux, 1967.

The Séance and Other Stories, translated by Roger Klein, Cecil Hemley, and others. New York: Farrar, Straus and Giroux, 1968.

UNCOLLECTED STORIES

"The Boudoir," *Vogue,* 147:148–49, 214 (April 1, 1966).

"The Colony," *Commentary,* 46:57–61 (November 1968).

"The Courtship," *Playboy,* 14:145, 200–2, 204, 206–7 (September 1967). (Excerpt from *The Manor.*)

"A Friend of Kafka," *New Yorker,* 44:59–63 (November 23, 1968).

"Hail, The Messiah," in *Jewish Short Stories of Today,* edited by Morris Kreitman. London: Faber and Faber, 1938. Pp. 35–51. (An abridged, variant version of *Satan in Goray*'s first six chapters.)

"My Adventures as an Idealist," *Saturday Evening Post,* 240:68–73 (November 18, 1967).

"Pigeons," *Esquire,* 68:76–79 (August 1967).

"Powers," *Harper's,* 235:76–78, 83–87 (October 1967).

"The Prodigal Fool," *Saturday Evening Post,* 239:64–66, 68–69 (February 26, 1966).

BEN SIEGEL

"The Riddle," *Playboy*, 14:164–66, 253–54 (January 1967).
"Yash the Chimney Sweep," *Saturday Evening Post*, 241:66, 68–69 (May 4, 1968).

MEMOIRS

"Dreamers," *Reporter*, 35:45–46 (July 14, 1966).
In My Father's Court, translated by Channah Kleinerman-Goldstein and others. New York: Farrar, Straus and Giroux, 1966.
"A Wedding," *Dimensions in American Judaism*, 2:15–16 (Fall 1967).

ARTICLES AND REVIEWS

"The Everlasting Joke," *Commentary*, 31:458–60 (May 1961).
"The Extreme Jews," *Harper's*, 234:55–62 (April 1967).
"Hagigah," *American Judaism*, 16:19, 48–49 (Winter 1966–67).
"Introduction" to *The Adventures of One Yitzchok* by Yitzchok Perlov. New York: Award Books, 1967. Pp. 7–12.
"Introduction" to *Hunger* by Knut Hamsun. New York: Noonday Press, 1968. Pp. v–xii.
"Introduction" to *Yoshe Kalb* by I. J. Singer. New York: Harper and Row, 1965. Pp. v–x.
"A New Use for Yiddish," *Commentary*, 33:267–69 (March 1962).
"Once on Second Avenue There Lived a Yiddish Theater," *New York Times*, April 17, 1966, Section 2, p. 3.
"Peretz' Dream," *American Judaism*, 15:20–21, 60–61 (Passover 1966).
"A Phantom of Delight," *Herald Tribune Book Week*, July 4, 1965, pp. 2, 7.
"The Poetry of Faith," *Commentary*, 32:258–60 (September 1961).
"Realism and Truth," *The Reconstructionist*, 28:5–9 (June 15, 1962).
"Rootless Mysticism," *Commentary*, 39:77–78 (January 1965).
"The Ten Commandments and the Modern Critics," *Cavalier*, June 1965, p. 30.
"What It Takes to Be a Jewish Writer," *National Jewish Monthly*, 78:54–56 (November 1963).
"What's in It for Me?" *Harper's*, 231:172–73 (October 1965).

CURRENT AMERICAN REPRINTS

The Family Moskat. New York: Bantam, $1.25; Noonday, $2.25.
Gimpel the Fool and Other Stories. New York: Avon, $.60; Noonday, $1.45.
In My Father's Court. New York: Signet (New American Library), $.95; Noonday, $1.95.
The Magician of Lublin. New York: Bantam, $.95; Noonday, $1.65.
Satan in Goray. New York: Avon, $.60; Noonday, $1.25.

Selected Short Stories. New York: Modern Library (Random House), $2.45.
Short Friday and Other Stories. New York: Signet, $.75; Noonday, $2.25.
The Slave. New York: Avon, $.75; Noonday, $1.95.
The Spinoza of Market Street. New York: Avon, $.60; Noonday, $1.95.

Critical and Biographical Studies

Angoff, Charles. "Aspects of American Literature," *Literary Review*, 10:5–17 (Autumn 1966).

Ash, Lee. "WLB Biography: Isaac Bashevis Singer," *Wilson Library Bulletin*, 37:356 (December 1962).

Blocker, Joel, and Richard Elman. "An Interview with Isaac Bashevis Singer," *Commentary*, 36:364–72 (November 1963).

Buchen, Irving. *Isaac Bashevis Singer and the Eternal Past.* New York: New York University Press, 1968.

Chametzky, Jules. "The Old Jew in New Times," *Nation*, 205:436–38 (October 30, 1967).

Eisenberg, J. A. "Isaac Bashevis Singer — Passionate Primitive or Pious Puritan," *Judaism*, 11:345–56 (Fall 1962).

Elman, Richard M. "The Spinoza of Canal Street," *Holiday*, 38:83–87 (August 1965).

Feldman, Irving. "The Shtetl World," *Kenyon Review*, 24:173–77 (Winter 1962).

Fixler, Michael. "The Redeemers: Themes in the Fiction of Isaac Bashevis Singer," *Kenyon Review*, 26:371–86 (Spring 1964).

Flender, Harold. "Isaac Bashevis Singer," *Paris Review*, 11:53–73 (Fall 1968).

Frank, M. Z. "The Demon and the Earlock," *Conservative Judaism*, 20:1–9 (Fall 1965).

Glanville, Brian. "An Interview with Isaac Bashevis Singer," *Jewish News*, September 28, 1962, p. 28.

Glatstein, Jacob. "The Fame of Bashevis Singer," *Congress Bi-Weekly*, 32:17–19 (December 27, 1965).

Goodheart, Eugene. "The Demonic Charm of Bashevis Singer," *Midstream*, 6:88–93 (Summer 1960).

Hemley, Cecil. "Isaac Bashevis Singer," in *Dimensions of Midnight: Poetry and Prose*, edited by Elaine Gottlieb. Athens: Ohio University Press, 1966 Pp. 217–33.

Hindus, Milton. "Isaac Bashevis Singer," in *Jewish Heritage Reader*, edited by Morris Adler. New York: Taplinger, 1965. Pp. 242–52.

Hochman, Baruch. "I. B. Singer's Vision of Good and Evil," *Midstream*, 13:66–73 (March 1967).

BEN SIEGEL

Howe, Irving. "Demonic Fiction of a Yiddish 'Modernist,'" *Commentary*, 30:350–53 (October 1960).

Hughes, Catharine R. "The Two Worlds of Isaac Singer," *America*, 117:611–13 (November 18, 1967).

Hughes, Ted. "The Genius of Isaac Bashevis Singer," *New York Review of Books*, April 22, 1965, pp. 8–10.

Hyman, Stanley Edgar. "Isaac Singer's Marvels," *New Leader*, 47:17–18 (December 21, 1964).

Jacobson, Dan. "The Problem of Isaac Bashevis Singer," *Commentary*, 39:48–52 (February 1965).

Kazin, Alfred. "The Saint as Schlemiel," in *Contemporaries*. Boston: Little, Brown, 1962. Pp. 283–91.

Leibowitz, Herbert. "A Lost World Redeemed," *Hudson Review*, 19:669–73 (Winter 1966–67).

Madison, Charles A. "I. Bashevis Singer: Novelist of Hasidic Gothicism," in *Yiddish Literature, Its Scope and Major Writers*. New York: Frederick Ungar, 1968. Pp. 479–99.

Malin, Irving, ed. *Critical Views of Isaac Bashevis Singer*. New York: New York University Press, 1969.

Mucke, Edith. "Isaac B. Singer and Hassidic Philosophy," *Minnesota Review*, 7:214–21 (Numbers 3 and 4, 1967).

Pondrom, Cyrena N. "Isaac Bashevis Singer: An Interview," *Contemporary Literature*, 10:1–38, 332–51 (Winter, Summer 1969).

Rexroth, Kenneth. "Alienated: Indomitable," *Commentary*, 26:458–60 (November 1958).

Roback, A. A. "The Singer Family," *Contemporary Yiddish Literature: A Brief Outline*. London: Lincolns-Prager, 1957. Pp. 63–71.

Siegel, Ben. "Sacred and Profane: Isaac Bashevis Singer's Embattled Spirits," *Critique*, 6:24–47 (Spring 1963).

Sloan, Jacob. "I. B. Singer and His Yiddish Critics," *Congress Bi-Weekly*, 33:4–5 (March 7, 1966).

Sloman, Judith. "Existentialism in Par Lagerkvist and Isaac Bashevis Singer," *Minnesota Review*, 5:206–12 (August–October 1965).

Sontag, Susan. "Demons and Dreams," *Partisan Review*, 29:460–63 (Summer 1962).

Teller, Judd L. "From Yiddish to Neo-Brahmin," in *Strangers and Natives*. New York: Delacorte, 1968. Pp. 262–65.

Wolkenfeld, J. S. "Isaac Bashevis Singer: The Faith of His Devils and Magicians," *Criticism*, 5:349–59 (Fall 1963).

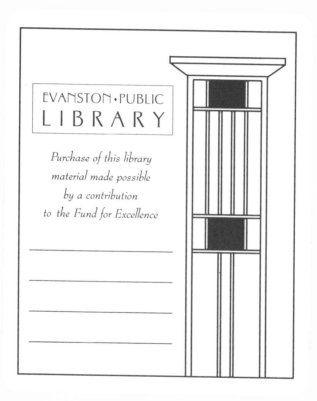